To Rosalie Wychinowski,

For the faith,

Don Tingle

# PHASES AND FACES OF THE MOON
## A CRITICAL EVALUATION
### OF THE
## UNIFICATION CHURCH AND ITS PRINCIPLES

# PHASES AND FACES OF THE MOON

## A CRITICAL EVALUATION OF THE UNIFICATION CHURCH AND ITS PRINCIPLES

Donald S. Tingle
and Richard A. Fordyce

EXPOSITION PRESS
HICKSVILLE, NEW YORK

FIRST EDITION

Library of Congress Catalog Card Number: 79-50738

ISBN 0-682-49264-7

Printed in the United States of America

To our wives, Linda and Jan,
who have provided much encouragement
along the way.

THROUGHOUT THIS BOOK Sun Myung Moon is referred to as Reverend Moon. The authors *only* use the title "Reverend" because it is the popular title by which his followers refer to him.

# Contents

The authors wrote to the Unification Church requesting permission to quote from their copyrighted material. Bruce A. Brown, Assistant Director of Legal Affairs, responded that "we do not at this time grant to you permission to reproduce any portion" of the Unification Church's copyrighted material. He also informed the authors that libel action is being brought against two publishing companies "for publications considered by us to be defamatory." Therefore, the authors have been forced to paraphrase as accurately as possible copyrighted Unification Church material. The ample supply of footnotes at the end of each chapter should provide the serious student adequate documentation of all references.

# Foreword
# by Dr. Byron Lambert

It was my privilege to be the moderator of a debate between the authors of this book and two representatives of the Unification Church on the evening of Tuesday, March 8, 1977. The debate is referred to only briefly in these pages, but so successful was it from the standpoint of Messrs. Tingle and Fordyce, that it encouraged their writing this book. The conditions and questions of the debate, together with the time limits for speeches and rebuttals, were all carefully worked out between the opposing sides before the event. All I had to do as moderator was make sure the participants observed the time limits and put the audience in the right frame of mind for the contest. The auditors were almost entirely from the Christian churches and Churches of Christ in the area, and they packed the rather spacious sanctuary

of the West Islip, New York, Church of Christ. It would have
been easy to put the followers of Sun Myung Moon at a
psychological disadvantage under the circumstances and so
contaminate the character of the debate, which brothers
Tingle and Fordyce wanted to win on purely rational
grounds. The audience, in my view, exhibited exemplary
Christian equity and restraint and observed all the rules of
courteous attention, especially as their ears were assaulted
with statements by the advocates of the Reverend Moon
which could not help but take their breath away.

I would like to state, also, that the debaters themselves
were models of fairness and decorum. They did not play to
the galleries, and they kept to the topics assigned and to
the time limits.

From what I have said one might wonder whether the
debate could arouse any interest, so accustomed are we to
viewing spurious television "debates" which amount to little
more than shouting matches between irascible and unthink-
ing opponents. The fact is, the atmosphere of the debate
fairly crackled with excitement—healthy excitement, the
kind of electric interest that charges every discussion where
truth is at stake and the combatants are men of courage and
rationality. Such an ambiance strengthens and exhilarates
audience and debater alike, and such was the experience on
that evening in March, 1977.

My first judgment about the debate grows stronger with
each passing month, and that is, *in a debate over biblical
principles, there is no substitute for knowing the Good Book.*
The two leaders of the Unification Church were surprisingly
weak in this respect, although both had backgrounds in seminary education, Episcopal and Roman Catholic, and in all

formal respects appeared to have the educational advantage. But they were no match for the two Church of Christ preachers, who not only knew their Scripture "cold," but had obviously done the better research in ferreting out the chinks in their opponents' armor, and showed far more labor (and this is a form of humility) in preparing for the evening than the Moon people had done. One wonders what the leaders of the Unification Church imagined they were coming up against.

The lesson of the debate is worth restating: *know your Bible.* This was the principle that put Alexander Campbell and the mighty pleaders for New Testament Christianity so far ahead of their adversaries in the early days of the Restoration Movement. And if there is ever a revival of debate among the Christian churches as one of the means to put the Plea before the world, our colleges and seminaries will have to emphasize day in and day out with the students the indispensability of knowing the Bible with an intimacy and love that puts every gainsayer to flight, or at least makes him think twice before issuing a challenge.

There is one matter I have not discussed with the authors of this book, and I wish to include it now. It occurred to me the night of the debate, but I did not mention it to them then; nor have I said anything since. The point is this: almost all of the attacks against the Unification Church in the public news media are directed against their so-called brain-washing techniques and the horrors of life going on in the inner sanctum of Reverend Moon's church. The furor and pressure created by the media are extremely dangerous, not just to the partisans of the *Divine Principle,* but to any group zealous to promote a religious cause. The accusations

cast a kind of slander on a young person's right to change
his religious faith or to work in an unpopular or not quite
traditional religious body, or to call door to door and dis-
tribute tracts, or to hold camps and religious retreats and
congregate with others in any "exclusive" way. The Moon
followers, in my estimation, are guilty of no more than
Jehovah's Witnesses, or Mormons, or (do I need to say it)
people of the Christian churches, when they seek to convert
others to their way. It was to the credit of brother Fordyce
and brother Tingle that they gave not the slightest hint of
demeaning the personal convictions and techniques of their
opponents; never once did they resort to the *ad hominem*
argument for the sake of arousing the biases of their audience. Nor did they do so in this book. The fact is, they are
instinctively, if I may so say, manifesting the grace that comes
from debating over issues of truth—and truth alone; and in
doing so they are protecting the right of rational human
beings to exercise their religious freedom as laid down in
the First Amendment of the Constitution. Most of those I
hear complaining about the "Moonies" don't have the slightest notion of how to meet their alien doctrines except by
political suppression and clamorous propaganda. In doing so
they encroach dangerously on a principle which protects us
all, and we do no good by joining in the ugly outcry.

The authors are to be commended by their aloofness
from the cheap techniques which I have just described and
which could give them only a synthetic victory over the
errors of Pastor Moon and his following.

There will be other Moons in the years to come, if the
Lord tarry, just as there have been Mohammeds and Joseph
Smiths in the past. But the follower of the Way has nothing

to fear so long as he holds the form of truth once delivered
to the saints. This book and the debate that engendered it
are proof of my point.

—BYRON C. LAMBERT, PH.D.
Director of Peter Sammartino College of Education,
Fairleigh Dickinson University,
Madison, New Jersey

# Introduction

Neil A. Salonen, President of the Unification Church of America, has stated,

> The Unification Church is absolutely a Christian movement. . . . Allegations that we are un-Christian can only be justified either by distortions of what we really teach or by the most narrow and sectarian definition of Christianity.[1]

The purpose of this study is to examine that claim. Can the Unification Church be called a Christian movement? (If they can, why have they been denied membership in the National Council of Churches?) More importantly, can one be a Christian and a follower of Sun Myung Moon at the same time?

This study is not a call for denying religious freedom

to Reverend Moon and his church as guaranteed by the First Amendment to the Constitution of the United States. The authors firmly believe in safeguarding religious freedom for all who desire to proclaim their faith honestly and honorably. The authors, however, desire the public's attention in examining whether or not the Unification Church is both honest and honorable in their claims. If they are Christian, their doctrine will prove it. If they are not Christian, they should cease from attempting to deceive the public.

Thomas Jefferson once said,

> Truth is great and will prevail if left to herself. . . . She is the proper and sufficient antagonist to error, and has nothing to fear from the conflict unless by human interposition disarmed of her natural weapons, free argument and debate; errors ceasing to be dangerous when it is permitted freely to contradict them.[2]

Reverend Moon and his church claim to be Christian and therefore have nothing to fear from a thorough examination of their teachings and practices in relation to the biblical claims of Christianity—unless they are attempting to mislead the public.

Jesus said that his ministry was not done in secrecy but was always open to public scrutiny.[3] He told his followers to be like a city set on a hill or a light for all to behold. Christianity was never to be an esoteric religion with secret teachings and rites, and thus it stood in contrast to contemporary mystery religions. How different the openness of Christianity is to the attitude of Reverend Moon and his followers who are often reluctant to reveal to the public many of their basic doctrines. When Jesus was asked if he were the Christ, he gave a direct answer in the affirmative.[4] When Reverend Moon was asked by reporters from *Newsweek* magazine if he were the new Christ or Messiah, he replied evasively, "Let God answer you, let God answer the world."[5] This book attempts to push the veil of secrecy aside for the reader.

This book is an outgrowth of a public debate the authors held with Kurt Johnson, Director of the Interfaith Affairs Committee of the Unification Movement (IACUM) and Shawn Byrne, Coordinator of IACUM, at the West Islip Church of Christ on Long Island, New York, in March of 1977. The authors were able to interview Susan Reinbold, National Director of Media Relations for the Unification Church, and Daniel Holdgreiwe, National Director of Public Affairs, before the debate. Dan and Sue gave the authors a tour of the national headquarters building and supplied them with numerous papers and several books of an authoritative nature concerning their church.

It is the fond hope of the authors that all who examine this book, as it compares Unification Church teaching with the Bible, will show the same integrity as those the apostle Paul met at Berea:

Now these Jews were more noble than those in Thessalonica, for they received the word with all eagerness, examining the scriptures daily to see if these things were so.[6]

DON TINGLE AND RICK FORDYCE
*Connecticut*

## NOTES

1. "A Statement by Neil A. Salonen," President, Unification Church of America, February 23, 1976, p. 5.
2. Brodie, *Thomas Jefferson, an Intimate History*, p. 155.
3. Jn. 18:20.
4. Jn. 10:24, 25.
5. *Newsweek,* international edition, June 14, 1976, p. 48.
6. Acts 17:11.

# PHASES AND FACES OF THE MOON
## A CRITICAL EVALUATION
### OF THE
## UNIFICATION CHURCH AND ITS PRINCIPLES

# ONE

# A Brief History

Sun Myung Moon was born January 6, 1920, in what is now North Korea. He was the fifth of eight children born to a Korean farmer. When he was ten years old his family became members of the Presbyterian Church in Korea. Moon's life changed dramatically, as he himself states: "I had a very strong desire to live a life of high dimension. When I was twelve years old, I started praying for extraordinary things. I asked for wisdom greater than Solomon's, for faith greater than the Apostle Paul's and for love greater than the love Jesus had."[1]

On Easter morning, 1936, Moon was visited by Jesus Christ in the Korean countryside. Jesus explained that Moon had been chosen to complete the task that Jesus had failed to complete—to establish the Kingdom of God on earth.

After much anguish and struggle, Moon accepted the challenge.

Over the next nine years Moon received revelations,
which have been incorporated into the *Divine Principle*, the
"Bible" of the Unification Church. "The revelation was received progressively through prayer, study of all religious
scriptures, meditation, spiritual communication with such
persons as Jesus, Moses and Buddha, and direct communication with God."[2] The revelations did not cease after the
nine years; as Moon himself says, "Ever since that particular
encounter (Easter, 1936), I have been in constant communication with the living God and the living saints in the
spirit world, including Jesus, in my own search for truth."[3]

Between 1946 and 1954 Moon preached his message at
various places in Korea and gathered together his disciples.
He endured several prison terms during these years. The
first was in August, 1946, when the "Communists arrested
him, tortured and beat him, and finally left him for dead."[4]
The other imprisonment was in February, 1948, when he
was again imprisoned by the Communists. After two and a
half years of hard labor and much suffering, he was again
released from prison.[5] During these years of torture in prison,
Moon revealed some of his attitudes toward God. "Rather
than seeking to be comforted, he sought to comfort God."[6]

In 1953 Moon moved to Seoul, and in 1954 he officially
formed the Holy Spirit Association for the Unification of
World Christianity. This association is more commonly
known as the Unification Church.

Also in 1954, Moon's wife of ten years left him. "When
Moon devoted his entire life to the work of the church
that was a commitment his [first] spouse couldn't sustain."[7]
In 1960 Moon married an eighteen-year-old high school

graduate named Hak Ja Han. The marriage between Moon and Hak Ja Han has been referred to as "the Marriage of the Lamb." Moon is called the "Father of the Universe" and Hak Ja Han is called the "Mother of the Universe."[8]

In 1965 the Korean church was strong enough for Moon to begin his worldwide campaign. In that first year he traveled to forty nations, including the United States.[9] Since that time, the worldwide headquarters for the Unification Church has been moved to New York City.

In 1976 the Unification Church claimed two million members, including 400,000 in South Korea, 260,000 in Japan, 30,000 in the United States, 6,000 in West Germany, 1,000 in France, 3,000 in Britain, and 2,000 in Holland.[10] Very simply, their goal is to unite the world under the teachings of Sun Myung Moon, thus hoping to bring the Kingdom of God to earth. It is that teaching of Moon which we propose to examine in the rest of this book, to see if his teaching will indeed bring the Kingdom of God to earth, or the kingdom of someone else.

## NOTES

1. "Sun Myung Moon," a booklet published by the Unification Church of America, New York, p. 25.
2. *Ibid.*
3. *Newsweek*, June 14, 1976, international edition, p. 48.
4. "Sun Myung Moon," p. 27.
5. There are several conflicting reports about Moon's imprisonments. For more information, see *The Puppet Master*, J. Isamu Yamamoto. pp. 17-19.
6. "Sun Myung Moon," p. 29.

7. A quote by Neil Salonen, the president of the Unification Church of America, in the *Newsweek* article, p. 46.
8. Yamamoto, p. 21. Mr. Yamamoto further mentions that some critics claim that Moon has been married four times, not just twice as he and his followers admit.
9. "Sun Myung Moon," p. 33.
10. *Newsweek*, p. 44.

# TWO

## *Final Authority*

Every group must have a final authority to which it always returns in deciding matters of controversy, opinion, or interpretation. Without a final authority, there is only confusion, and the door to chaos is left open.

Since the Unification Church claims that it is an absolutely Christian movement and that the Bible plays a central role in their teaching,[1] one would expect their doctrines to be based upon and agree with the Bible. One would further expect the Unification Church to regard the Bible as God's word to His people. As one reads literature from their church, however, it becomes clear that they only pay lip service to the Bible without using it as a reliable authority. They claim that since the Bible is not complete, a new expression of truth will need to appear.[2]

Their attitude toward the Bible is well expressed in this quote:

> We believe that the Bible is more the record of the actions of those people whom God inspired. We definitely believe that the sayings of Paul and the words of the apostles to the early Christians were inspired of God. And, therefore, we believe that the Bible is substantially God's word. But we don't believe that God has been victorious in every interchurch fight over what should and what should not be the Biblical position.[3]

One can honestly agree that not every church controversy has been settled in full agreement with God's word, but problems arise when the credibility of Christianity's final authority is weakened by calling the Bible "substantially" God's word and deny that it is "perfect and absolute in itself." It seems their beliefs are based on the passages of scripture which God either lost or had not revealed, because they certainly are not based on the Bible.

The Unification Church teaches that Reverend Moon is a spokesman for God to the world and is the most important religious prophet of this age.[4] A prophet is a person who receives his message directly from God. Since God does not lie and is not a God of confusion or contradiction, one prophet's message will not contradict the message of any other prophet of God.

So what happens when the beliefs of this new prophet are compared with a substantially correct Bible, which plays a central role in their very Christian position? Confusion and contradiction arise everywhere! Their teachings are at odds with the revealed word of God.

One of the most important doctrines of the Unification Church is the fall of man. Although this doctrine will be studied in more detail later, it is necessary to introduce it here to show what has been done with God's word. The Unification Church teaches that sin originated on earth when Eve had sexual relations with Lucifer. Realizing her mistake, she then tried to become perfect again by having sexual relations with Adam. This act only complicated the matter, because Adam and Eve were in the process of becoming perfect; they were not yet husband and wife but were only in a brother-sister relationship. So instead of being made perfect again, Eve caused Adam to sin, completing both a spiritual and a physical fall.[5] The only similarity this account has with the Bible is that it mentions the same characters. The Bible teaches that God created a perfect, not an imperfect, immature world, as the Unification Church teaches. Furthermore, the Bible teaches that "the man and his *wife* were both naked, and were not ashamed,"[6] and this describes their relationship *before* the fall, not after it. Not only does Moon change the nature of the fall, but he also says that man was created for the sake of the woman.[7] Does this agree with God's explanation in Genesis 2:18-25?

In explaining why Moses was unable to lead the people into the Promised Land, the *Divine Principle*, the "Bible" of the Unification Church, says Moses struck the rock twice instead of once.[8] Yet Numbers 20:8-12, which is given as a reference in *Divine Principle*, clearly states that Moses was to speak to the rock, not strike it.

Concerning John the Baptist, Reverend Moon explains that John did not live on locusts and wild honey alone, because Israel doesn't yield much honey today; therefore

Moon concludes, John must have gone from house to house as a beggar.[9]

Where does Reverend Moon get these ideas? He claims that since there is so much which the Bible does not teach, Jesus and God have revealed some amazing secrets to him.[10]

Apparently the only role the Bible has in the doctrinal position of the Unification Church is to be quoted and referred to sufficiently so that they will have the appearance of being Christian. The Bible is clearly not their final authority. This is evident in their misuse of the Bible and also in their attitude toward their book, *Divine Principle,* which they say is the "fundamental guide" to reach God and is a standard by which God restores sinful man.[11] This *Divine Principle,* God's new expression of truth, is to unite all Christendom and all civilizations of the world.

Can the Bible play a central role in a church with the above statement as a major belief? If it can, then what should be done with these statements from the Bible?

Jesus said, ". . . and I, when I am lifted up from the earth, will draw all men to *myself.*"[12]

When the Spirit of truth comes, he will guide you into *all* the truth.[13]

So faith comes from what is heard, and what is heard comes by the preaching of *Christ.*[14]

All scripture is inspired by God and profitable for teaching, for reproof, for correction, and for training in righteousness, that the man of God may be *complete*, equipped for *every* good work.[15] [This indicates that the Bible contains EVERYTHING necessary for salvation and spiritual growth.]

I found it necessary to write appealing to you to contend for the faith which was *once for all* delivered to the saints.[16] [Therefore, no new faith can be given.]

I am astonished that you are so quickly deserting him who called you in the grace of Christ and turning to a different gospel—not that there is another gospel, but there are some who trouble you and want to pervert the gospel of Christ. But even if we, or an angel from heaven, should preach to you a gospel contrary to that which we preached to you, let him be accursed. As we have said before, so now I say again, If any one is preaching to you a gospel contrary to that which you received, let him be accursed.[17]

Clearly, the Unification Church does not accept the Bible as their final authority for faith and practice. Then is it possible for them to be an absolutely Christian movement, with the Bible playing a central role in their teaching?

In a word, NO!

## NOTES*

1. President Salonen, "A Statement," February 23, 1976, p. 5.
2. *Divine Principle*, p. 9.
3. Authors' private interview with Daniel C. Holdgreiwe, Director of Public Affairs for the Unification Church.

---

*Italics in Biblical quotations have been added by authors for emphasis.

4. President Salonen, "A Statement," January 12, 1976, p. 6.
5. *Divine Principle*, pp. 65-80.
6. Gen. 2:25. Italics added for emphasis.
7. *New Hope*, p. 16.
8. *Divine Principle*, pp. 325, 326.
9. *New Hope*, p. 4.
10. *A Prophet Speaks Today*, p. 138.
11. *New Hope*, pp. 32, 33.
12. Jn. 12:32.
13. Jn. 16:13.
14. Rom. 10:17.
15. 2 Tim. 3:16, 17.
16. Jude 3.
17. Gal. 1:6-9.

# THREE

## Theology of a Weak God

The basic doctrines of any religion are conditioned by that religion's concept of God. If its theology of God is faulty, the rest of its doctrines naturally are distorted. At first glance one might suppose the Unification Church to adhere to the Judaeo-Christian tradition as revealed in the Bible. They claim, "We believe in one personal God."[1] But do they believe in the same personal God who has spoken through the Bible?

Reverend Moon has adapted the Oriental concept of Yin and Yang (negative and positive aspects of nature) to show that God must exist as dual essentialities, positive and negative. God as spirit (positive and masculine) created the universe to be His feminine (negative) counterpart.[2] Reverend Moon further teaches that God has symbolically pro-

35

jected Himself in creation. Creation is God incarnate.[3] This appears to be a pantheism which basically teaches that the universe is God or each part is a manifestation of God.

The Bible from Genesis 1:1 on teaches that God created man and the universe as separate and distinct entities from Himself. The universe is not an extension of God; neither is it a body for His spirit. The heavens declare the glory of God;[4] man was made in the image of God;[5] God can fill all things;[6] but there always exists a distinction between the Creator and the created—one is not an extension of the other. One reason God forbade the use of any graven images was to show that He was Creator and not part of creation.[7]

In the principle of Yang and Yin, a good God would of necessity have an evil counterpart. The theology of Reverend Moon reflects this by proclaiming a weak God and a strong Satan. Reverend Moon places Satan in a position of equal bargaining power with God when he says that God must accept a standard of judgment which is also acceptable to Satan.[8] The scriptures never allowed for this equality. Satan stands condemned before God and has no bargaining power whatsoever. How can one who fell from heaven[9] and has been condemned to a time of eternal torment[10] have the leverage to demand a standard of judgment which he can approve? Instead of affirming the total sovereignty of God which the Bible portrays (especially in Romans and Revelation), Reverend Moon displays a God who has become resentful, sorrowful, and disillusioned[11] as He views the way a mighty devil has effectively thwarted His plans throughout history.

Unification theology teaches that God has lost His sovereignty.[12] He is invisible and so cannot do everything He wants. He needs you, and without you He can do nothing.[13] In fact, without you He cannot even be happy.[14] Therefore, as Reverend Moon assesses the mess God's plans are in, he says, that God is to be pitied.[15] It is better to comfort God and calm his nerves than to request His help.[16]

How different this is from the God of the Bible! The Psalmist contrasts man's foolish rebellion with the sovereignty of God by saying,

> Why do the nations conspire,
> and the peoples plot in vain?
> The kings of the earth set themselves,
> and the rulers take counsel together,
> against the Lord and his anointed, saying,
> "Let us burst their bonds assunder,
> and cast their cords from us."
> He who sits in the heavens laughs;
> the Lord has them in derision.
> Then he will speak to them in his wrath,
> and terrify them in his fury, saying,
> "I have set my king
> on Zion, my holy hill."[17]

The apostle Paul in speaking to the men of Athens concerning the Unknown God said, "Nor is he served by human hands, as though he needed anything, since he himself gives to all men life and breath and everything."[18] The true God, unlike Reverend Moon's concept, needs nothing from man

—not pity, not comfort, not advice. God is truly sovereign.

Man is not the strong one; God is. But Reverend Moon compounds his error when he says that a true son can tell God, "I am better than you, Father," and God will be "delighted" with the little boaster.[19] If a true son were of a superior nature, God would not expect the son to change the way he is praying just to suit Him.[20] In the present age it is not "Father knows best." Reverend Moon teaches that in past ages God may have guided man, but today a son is free to do things by himself.[21] In this work on God's behalf a true son not only has to second guess God,[22] but he also must become more serious than God in accomplishing His purposes.[23]

Reverend Moon's theology weakens his straw God and brings Him under the control of at least two forces. First, as can be guessed, God can be controlled by a truly loving son.[24] Second, God is tied down to numbers. Large portions of the *Divine Principle* dealing with restoration and Reverend Moon's commentary upon it are based on mathematical speculation. Everything in the Bible is interpreted symbolically, especially various numbers such as three, seven, and forty. Now, it is true that certain numbers have symbolic significance, but not to the extent which Reverend Moon carries things. The reader has heard the old saying, "The third time is the charm." Well, Reverend Moon carries the idea so far that he teaches that God had to establish a certain work by any means possible, because it was the third attempt.[25]

Then is God absolute or sovereign in any respect? Reverend Moon would answer yes. God is absolute in one respect

and one respect only—love.[26] The apostle John agrees that
"God is love,"[27] but John does not say that it is the only thing
God is. God is love, and He is much more than love. He is
also sovereign. So Reverend Moon shortchanges God's honor.

One of the best ways to counteract Moon's concept of a
weak God is to examine the various names and titles by
which He has revealed Himself. Although space prohibits
a full study of these names, even a surface examination
reveals the God of the Bible is not the same as Moon's
weak God.

*Elohim* is the ordinary name used for God in the Hebrew
Old Testament.[28] This plural word sometimes denotes hea-
then gods, but when it was used with reference to the one
true God it showed the fullness of His nature, majesty, and
power. Since a singular word for God was not always adequate to express His unsurpassed greatness, the plural word
*Elohim* was often used.

*El*, though similar in appearance, is probably not related
philologically to *Elohim*. *El* can be interpreted as the "strong
one" or "the ruler." It has no connection with Moon's weak
God that needs to be pitied. *El* emphasizes the power and
authority of God.

*El* was oftentimes combined with other words to show
various aspects of God's majesty. *El Shaddai* is a common
appellation for God in the Old Testament. Although the
meaning of *Shaddai* is uncertain, the title has been translated as "God Almighty" since nearly three hundred years
before the birth of Christ.[29] It is similar in meaning to the
Greek word *pantokrator* in the New Testament. *Pantokrator*

is used with reference to God alone and is translated as "Almighty" or "Ruler of All."[30] This word was also used in the Septuagint as a translation of "the Lord of Hosts,"[31] signifying God's total power and rule over all authorities, including the armies of heaven.

The most common proper name used for God was *Yahweh*,[32] which was associated with the Hebrew verb "to be." When Moses requested God to reveal His name, God replied from the burning bush, "I AM WHO I AM,"[33] which was the essential meaning of the name *Yahweh*. The name signified more than absolute existence, past, present, and future; it revealed a God who always stepped into history as a timely helper. Moon would lead us to believe that in times past God has ruled only indirectly;[34] God would have us realize that He is available in times of trouble.[35]

The name *Yahweh*, because of its most sacred nature, eventually was spoken only by the High Priest as he performed his ministry in the temple. All others substituted the word *Adonai* for the sacred name. *Adonai* meant "Lord," and referred to God's absolute rule over the created universe. In most Old Testament translations, Lord is used instead of Yahweh, and throughout the New Testament the inspired writers used the title Lord for God.

The Bible is filled with many other references showing the absolute sovereignty of God. Any honest Bible student is confronted immediately with numerous scriptures showing that the Creator is not weakened by or subjected to any created being.

The God that Sun Myung Moon and the Unification Church proclaim is a weak God for the following reasons:

1. Their God appears to be pantheistic.
2. They claim their God has lost His sovereignty.
3. Satan has equal bargaining power with their God.
4. They teach that a true son can claim to be better than God and can control Him.
5. Their God is controlled by numbers.

## *NOTES*

1. President Salonen, "A Statement," February 23, 1976, p. 5.
2. *Divine Principle,* pp. 25-27.
3. *A Prophet Speaks Today,* p. 3.
4. Ps. 19:1.
5. Gen. 1:26.
6. Eph. 4:6.
7. Ex. 20:4.
8. *New Hope,* p. 31.
9. Lk. 10:18.
10. Rev. 20:10.
11. *New Hope,* p. 40.
12. *Unification Theology* . . . , p. 40.
13. *A Prophet Speaks Today,* p. 11.
14. *Ibid.,* p. 4.
15. *New Hope,* p. 39.
16. *A Prophet Speaks Today,* p. 157.
17. Ps. 2:1-6.
18. Acts 17:25.
19. *A Prophet* . . . , p. 49.

20. *New Hope*, p. 69.
21. *Ibid.*, p. 8.
22. *Ibid.*, p. 73.
23. *Ibid.*, p. 71.
24. *Ibid.*, p. 29.
25. *Divine Principle*, p. 394.
26. *New Hope*, p. 27.
27. 1 Jn. 4:16.
28. Gen. 1:1.
29. Num. 24:16 and Job 5:17 in the Septuagint.
30. 2 Cor. 6:18. Cf. Vine, *Expository Dictionary of New Testament Words,* p. 48.
31. Jer. 5:14.
32. Gen. 4:26.
33. Ex. 3:14.
34. *Divine Principle*, p. 55.
35. Ps. 46:1.

# FOUR

## *Is Jesus God?*

Any religion that claims to be Christian must naturally hold many doctrines in common with the New Testament accounts. The Unification Church teaches that Jesus Christ was God's son, that he actually came in the flesh, and that his purpose was to restore a lost world to the Father. Thus they appear to be Christian; however, as will be shown, the Unification Church not only rejects many of the biblical teachings concerning Jesus Christ, but they also contradict their own teachings on basic christological points.

Is Jesus Christ God? In one place, the *Divine Principle* does not deny that Jesus is God, and yet in another place it does deny that Jesus is God.[2] So it would appear the matter is settled in their own minds to disagree with the Father who named Jesus "Emmanuel" (which means, God with

43

us).[3] Part of their rationale for assuming Jesus is not God is that He would have come sooner, if he were God in human flesh.[4]

Every follower of Sun Myung Moon who knows his doctrine well must say that Jesus is not God; but they have to grapple with two difficult passages in the *Divine Principle*. In one place it says ". . . Jesus placed himself on the same level as God (Jn. 14:9) . . ."[5] Now how can Jesus be on the same level as God without being God's equal or God Himself? In a second passage the matter is complicated even more when the *Divine Principle* states without reservation that "Jesus is God in the flesh."[6] This passage does not say that Jesus served "as" God to the people in the same way Moses did, or that Jesus stood in God's place accomplishing His will; it simply says "Jesus is God in the flesh." If this is merely a problem of translation from the original Korean, the text should be corrected as soon as possible to avoid confusion on this important issue.

To say that Jesus is not God conflicts with the biblical position. Jesus Christ was fully man and fully God. Paul, in writing to the Philippians, shows that Jesus, who existed in the form of God, did not count equality with God a thing to be grasped. Since Jesus by his very nature existed as God, he had no need to grasp what already belonged to him. Instead, he "emptied himself, taking the form of a servant, being born in the likeness of men."[7] So while he was upon the earth he laid aside his divine rights and power. He could say "the Father is greater than I"[8] and "the Son can do nothing of his own accord, but only what he sees the Father doing,"[9] because he fully tasted of servitude as a human being.

Although Jesus laid aside his divine rights, he never lost

his divine nature. Isaiah prophesied Jesus would be called "Mighty God, Everlasting Father,"[10] the same titles by which God the Father is referred to in the Old Testament. When Jesus called himself "I am,"[11] his enemies picked up stones to throw at him, because they believed he blasphemed, realizing he had openly confessed that he was Yahweh or Jehovah God of the Hebrew scriptures.[12] Thomas, when he fell at the feet of the resurrected Jesus, called him, "My Lord and my God!"[13] Even God the Father addressed Jesus, saying, "Thy throne, O God, is for ever and ever."[14] Isaiah, Thomas, Paul, Jesus himself, and the heavenly Father have all declared that Jesus is God, and yet the *Divine Principle* declares that Jesus "can by no means be called God Himself."

In a public debate with the authors of this book, Kurt Johnson (Director of the Interfaith Affairs Committee of the Unification Movement) tried to sidestep the issue by saying, "Jesus was God. The question is, How was Jesus God?" That is like saying that Kurt is human, but how is he human? Or a rose is a rose, but how is it a rose? There is no logical way the full divinity of Jesus can be sidestepped by this question. Jesus is God, because that is his nature. Jesus is not simply like God, or godly, or only a representative of God; he is God Himself.[15]

Also, in other respects Reverend Moon's concept of Jesus Christ is less than scriptural. In one place he calls Jesus God's "only son,"[16] whereas in another place he calls Jesus God's "first son" with the commentator explaining that "the spiritual wholeness that Jesus achieved is the destiny of all persons."[17] The Unification Church teaches that Jesus became God's son by a devout life of service, instead of being born an individual who by his very nature was unique from all the rest of mankind throughout history.

It is true that Jesus Christ shared in our humanity, and therefore he can call us "brethren." But the New Testament clearly shows that Jesus is God's son in an entirely different sense than we could ever be. The apostle John uses the Greek word *huios,* or "son," for Jesus alone, and calls the rest of those who belong to God *teknon,* or "children." This is not always apparent in English translations, but John throughout his writings makes a sharp distinction between Jesus' nature and ours. This is why John calls Jesus God's "only begotten" son, which literally means "the only one of his kind." Jesus is the only one of his kind, because he dwelt on earth being fully God and fully man. The nature of Jesus Christ as the son of the Father is one which could never be matched by us. Jesus is God's only begotten son, and we are children by adoption. Jesus was never adopted.

Reverend Moon also says that Jesus is the fruit of God's Logos.[18] "Logos" is a Greek word found in John 1:1, and it means, "word, the reason and thought behind words, and the personal and rational sustainer of the universe." Now, Reverend Moon would have us believe that Jesus is the fruit or by-product of the Logos, but John says that the Logos "became flesh and dwelt among us,"[19] specifically showing that Jesus is the Logos. One reason why Reverend Moon does not call Jesus the Logos is because John says that "the Logos was with God, and the Logos was God."[20] This is one of many places where Reverend Moon adapts scriptural terms to his unscriptural theology.

Other discrepancies are obvious. Reverend Moons says that a religious leader (mediator) in his work of connecting God and man must belong to both sides and also *neither* side.[21] This contradicts Paul's declaration to Timothy that there is only "one mediator between God and men, the man

Christ Jesus."[22] No other religious leader can serve as a mediator for Christians. Jesus Christ did not fit Moon's description of a mediator as "belonging to both sides and neither side," because he was always totally on the Father's side.

Reverend Moon also teaches that we must respect and even worship such men as Noah, Abraham, Moses, John the Baptist, and other dispensational figures.[23] Jesus, however, told the devil that man must not worship any spirits or human beings when he said, "You shall worship the Lord your God and him only shall you serve."[24] The word for "serve" here can also be translated as "worship"; the word is used in a strictly religious sense referring to the performance of religious duties. So the commandment states that we cannot worship anyone other than God Himself. None of the dispensational figures mentioned above can receive our worship.

Jesus Christ is the only human being that God has sanctioned for other human beings to worship. The wise men worshipped the child Jesus,[25] the Gerasene demoniac worshipped the man Jesus,[26] and the disciples worshipped the resurrected Jesus.[27] The only reason why Jesus can and must be worshipped is because he is God Himself.

Naturally, the Unification Church cannot accept the virgin birth of Jesus if they reject his full divinity. God cannot be the only Father of Jesus; some human being must have physically united with Mary to form the child Jesus. Who would this man be? Young Oon Kim, the professor of systematic theology at the Unification Theological Seminary in New York, says that the suggestion of Zechariah being the father of Jesus has an intriguing quality about it. Then

Jesus could carry both Aaron's priestly lineage through Zechariah and David's royal lineage through Mary.[28] Professor Kim has really used her imagination in this theory. She says that the New Testament contains no evidence against such an idea, automatically dismissing the two gospel accounts of the virgin birth. The idea of old Zechariah seducing a teenage girl named Mary would be comical if it were not so blasphemous. Zechariah couldn't believe the angel's news that he and Elizabeth would have a son named John, because he was an old man;[29] therefore, how could he begin to think he could sin with Mary. The idea is preposterous. It takes more faith to believe that Zechariah was the father of Jesus than to believe in the virgin birth.

Reverend Moon not only denies Jesus' divinity and rejects the virgin birth, but he also tries to discredit Jesus' moral credibility. Reverend Moon says that since the Bible does not say much about Jesus' life before his public ministry, it could not have been a glorious life to record.[30] This totally contradicts the writer of Hebrews who says that Jesus "in every respect has been tempted as we are, yet without sinning."[31] It also contradicts all available evidence of Jesus' childhood concerning his experience at twelve years of age in the temple, and the fact that he "increased in wisdom and in stature, and in favor with God and man."[32] This is a glorious record, even if it is brief.

### NOTES

1. *Divine Principle*, p. 209.
2. *Divine Principle*, pp. 210, 211.
3. Matt. 1:23.

4. *Unification Theology & Christian Thought*, p. 147.
5. *Divine Principle*, p. 155.
6. *Ibid.*, p. 292.
7. Phil. 2:5-7.
8. Jn. 14:28.
9. Jn. 5:19.
10. Is. 9:6.
11. Jn. 8:58.
12. Ex. 3:14.
13. Jn. 20:28.
14. Heb. 1:8.
15. *See* Rev. 1:8, 17-18.
16. Moon, "God's Hope for America," June 1, 1976, delivered at Yankee Stadium.
17. *Sun Myung Moon*, p. 9.
18. *New Hope*, p. 32.
19. Jn. 1:14.
20. Jn. 1:1. Logos is translated "Word" in RSV.
21. *A Prophet Speaks Today*, p. 41.
22. 1 Tim. 2:5.
23. *New Hope*, p. 2.
24. Mt. 4:10.
25. Mt. 2:11.
26. Mk. 5:6.
27. Mt. 28:17.
28. *Unification Theology & Christian Thought*, p. 131.
29. Lk. 1:18.
30. *A Prophet Speaks Today*, p. 132.
31. Heb. 4:15.
32. Lk. 2:52.

# FIVE

# Sin and Salvation

Since the Unification Church rejects the authority of the Bible, teaches the theology of a weak God, and concludes that God is a failure, it is to be expected that their doctrine of sin and salvation will also differ from what God has revealed in His Word. The reader will not be disappointed. The Unification Church teaches a doctrine of sin and salvation as unique and original as their other doctrines.

According to the Unification Church, sin began in the world with the fall in the Garden of Eden. From that point, the story has been changed, only the names have remained the same.

The *Divine Principle* teaches that God created the world, but it was not a perfect world. Adam and Eve were in a brother/sister relationship. Once they became perfect, they were to become husband and wife and produce a family centered on God. However, Lucifer, disguised as a serpent, appeared in the Garden, seduced Eve, and had sexual relations with her. This act resulted in the spiritual fall of mankind. Realizing what she had done, Eve then seduced Adam, hoping to be perfected by him. But since they were only brother/sister and not husband/wife, their sexual relations resulted in the physical fall of mankind. (The reason given, by which one can know these sexual relations were sinful, is that Adam and Eve sewed fig leaves together to cover their sexual parts. If the sin were really eating the fruit of a tree, they would have covered their hands and mouths.) [1]

The *Divine Principle* further classifies sin into four kinds.[2] The first is man's original sin, which is the sin derived from the spiritual fall of Adam and Eve. Second is hereditary sin, which is transmitted to the descendants through the blood lineage.[3] Exodus 20:5 is given as a reference to illustrate this kind of sin. The third kind of sin is collective sin whereby no one individual is guilty, but everyone as a whole is. The crucifixion of Jesus is given as an example of collective sin. Finally, there is individual sin, which each person commits himself. Moon further teaches that if man could ever rid himself of the original sin, all the others would disappear as well. But no one has yet been found who could do that.[4]

In addition to the four kinds of sin, there are also at least two unforgivable sins, murder and adultery.[5]

The Unification Church differentiates between sin and blame; i.e., a person may commit a sin and yet still be considered blameless by God.[6] For example, Jacob's deception of Isaac and Esau is sinful because deception is against honesty and is therefore sinful. However, Jacob's deception was also necessary to fulfil God's will for Jacob. Since God had attempted to fulfil His will in so many other ways and failed,[7] He must now resort to trickery and deception. In this case sin was necessary to fulfil God's will.[8] Therefore, even though Jacob sinned, God considered him blameless.[9]

In one of his sermons, Moon created the situation in which a follower of God must either obey God (resulting in God's will not being accomplished) or disobey God (to fulfil God's will). Then Moon says that even if the son disobeyed, God would be proud and not angry.[10]

Sin entered the world, and all men are sinners. Because of sin man is separated from God and needs salvation. The Unification Church prefers the word "restoration" to salvation because they see salvation as restoring man to his condition before the fall in the Garden of Eden. Their terminology is acceptable, but their explanation is not, when compared to the Bible.

The *Divine Principle* teaches that God is partly responsible for man's fall.[11] (After all, if God had never created Adam and Eve, they never could have sinned!) Because He is partly responsible, God has felt compelled to restore man to his original status before the fall.[12] However, man must establish the condition by which God can restore him.[13] The setting up of such conditions is called "indemnity."[14]

Since man must save himself, the reader may wonder how Jesus fits into the picture. Jesus was God's latest attempt at restoring man. (All other attempts had failed.) His purpose was to establish the Kingdom of Heaven on earth,[15] marry, and produce the perfect family centered on God.[16] Before all this could be accomplished, the disbelieving Jews took Jesus and crucified him, thus spoiling God's plan.

(According to the *Divine Principle*, the crucifixion was not part of God's plan.[17]) Though the death of Jesus did not accomplish God's plan of liquidating man's original sin,[18] it at least provided man with spiritual salvation.[19]

So what the world is in is a predicament. God wants to save the world but cannot. Jesus tried to save the world but only half succeeded. Therefore, we must restore ourselves; we, instead of God, are to recreate ourselves.[20] Then we must turn from Satan and to God on our own.[21]

As already stated above, man comes back to God through indemnity. There are three conditions of indemnity according to the *Divine Principle*.[22] One is equal indemnity, setting the condition at an identical value to what was lost. The "eye for an eye and tooth for a tooth" idea is given as an example of equal indemnity.

A second condition is lesser indemnity, setting the condition at a value less than what was originally lost. According to this idea, we receive the identical salvation Jesus received[23] by setting up the condition of indemnity of baptism (sprinkling a few drops of water on our heads) and communion.

The third condition is greater indemnity, setting the condition at a price greater than what was originally lost. This indemnity enables one to "catch up" on conditions of indemnity missed previously. As an example, they cite Abraham's offering of Isaac. Since Abraham had failed when he offered sacrifices of a dove, ram, and heifer, he had to make up for it by offering his son Isaac.

People today must set a greater condition of indemnity because they must not only make indemnity for themselves but also for what was left undone by persons who lived previously.[24] And if indemnity is not completed in this life, there is always the spirit world to come to complete indemnity and pay for injustices.[25]

In the Unification Church today indemnity takes many forms—nothing as extreme as offering human sacrifices, since there is no perfect being to offer to Satan in return for freedom. But there are other forms. Prayer is a form of indemnity. Recruiting new followers is another, as is fund raising, Bible reading, studying Moon's teaching, and a list of things too numerous to mention.[26] In short, indemnity is anything you want to make it, since you establish the conditions. The zeal and enthusiasm of the Unification Church members is not so much based on love for God as it is compulsion to indemnify one's own sins. What they really have is a salvation based on work. The more one works the better chance one has of saving himself and others as well.

Salvation in the Unification Church is universal. The Kingdom of Heaven is the destination of us all.[27] When the Unification Church teaches that salvation is universal, they mean universal. For God to be completely triumphant, he must restore even the rebellious Satan.[28]

On the evening before their public debate with two leaders of the Unification Church, the authors had dinner with the two and others from the Church. One of the Church members described the final scene of Satan's return like this. Eventually everyone will be restored to God, and Satan will be all by himself. He will see all the love centered upon God, and Satan will finally walk up to God, humbly stand before Him, and in a very childish voice, say, "I'm sorry. Please take me back." God will receive Satan into Heaven, and God will again be completely in charge of His creation.

The Unification Church teaching on sin and salvation is confusing to many people. Many of the same words are used but the meanings have been changed. The teaching sounds biblical, yet a closer look reveals that the Unification Church doctrine of sin and salvation is unbiblical.

When God looked at the world He had created, the only thing that saddened Him was that the man was alone. God said, "It is not good that the man should be alone; I will make him a helper fit for him."[29] God created the woman for the man, looked at His creation and, "saw everything that he had made, and behold, it was very good."[30] Regarding the relationship of Adam and Eve, the Bible clearly states "the man and his *wife* were both naked, and were not ashamed."[31] Nowhere are Adam and Eve regarded as either imperfect or brother and sister. God created a perfect world. Adam and Eve were always husband and wife, before and after the fall.

The Bible nowhere indicates that Eve and Satan had any kind of sexual relationship. The serpent tempted Eve, she ate the fruit, then gave to her *husband* and he ate.[32] As a result of their actions, sin entered the world and perfection was gone. To find anything sexual in the biblical account of the fall is to read between lines that are not even there.

The Bible teaches from beginning to end that sin is the result of men rejecting God's authority. God had said, "You may freely eat of every tree of the garden; but of the tree of the knowledge of good and evil you shall not eat, for in the day that you eat of it you shall die."[33] When Adam and Eve ate, they rejected God's law and authority. "Everyone who commits sin is guilty of lawlessness; sin is lawlessness."[34] And there is no one to blame for sin but oneself. Adam and Eve each tried to "pass the buck" to someone else, but God holds each person responsible for his own sin. James says, "Let no one say when he is tempted, 'I am tempted by God'; for

God cannot be tempted with evil and he himself tempts no one; but each person is tempted when he is lured and enticed by his own desire."[35] God cannot be held responsible for the sin of Adam and Eve, not even partially.

According to the Bible, sin is sin. It is not divided into four kinds. The only kind of original sin in the Bible is the first sin committed by Eve. After that one, no more were original. But mankind in general is not guilty before God because of the original sin. "Sin came into the world through one man and death through sin, and so death spread to all men because all men sinned—"[36] All men die because of Adam's and their own sins, but not all men are sinners because of Adam.

Original sin is not derived from Adam, and neither is hereditary sin. "The soul that sins shall die. The son shall not suffer for the iniquity of the father, nor the father suffer for the iniquity of the son; the righteousness of the righteous shall be upon himself, and the wickedness of the wicked shall be upon himself."[37] It is true that sometimes a child will suffer physical results from the sins of parents. For example, children of drug-addicted mothers are often born addicts. But God says that no person suffers eternally for the sins of others. Each person is judged for his own sins.

It sometimes seems that the entire nation of Israel is considered guilty for the crucifixion of Jesus. As a nation they rejected Jesus, but each person must accept his own responsibility. As Peter spoke to many of those who had cried for Jesus' crucifixion, he said, "You [plural], with the help of wicked men, put him to death by nailing him to the cross."[38] When the people were pierced to the heart and asked what they could do, Peter replied, "Repent, and let each of you be baptized . . ."[39] indicating that each person was individually responsible for his own actions. No one was permitted to pass his guilt off onto the whole nation.

The only sin the Bible teaches is individual sin. However, there is a category of unforgivable sin, not the two sins advocated by the Unification Church. According to Jesus, "every sin and blasphemy will be forgiven men, but the blasphemy against the Spirit will not be forgiven."[40] No where is blasphemy against the Spirit equated with murder and adultery.

To say that Jesus did not complete salvation for the world is to miss the most important and obvious teaching in all the revealed Word of God. Just a few of the passages which teach complete salvation through Christ are cited below.

> . . . and you shall call his name Jesus, for he will save his people from their sins.[41]

> For the Son of man came to seek and to save the lost.[42]

> The saying is sure and worthy of full acceptance, that Christ Jesus came into the world to save sinners.[43]

> When Jesus had received the vinegar, he said, "It is finished"; and he bowed his head and gave up his spirit.[44]

> And there is salvation in no one else, for there is no other name under heaven given among men by which we must be saved.[45]

> For there is one God, and there is one mediator between God and men, the man Christ Jesus, who gave himself as a ransom for all, the testimony to which was borne at the proper time.[46]

. . . and the blood of Jesus his Son cleanses us from all sin.[47]

Jesus accomplished His mission. The writer of Hebrews states that Jesus has been sacrificed once for all, and has now sat down at the right hand of God.[48]

God not only wants to save man and restore his lost image to him, God has also provided the way through Jesus Christ. And God has set the conditions, not man. Salvation is only through faith in and obedience to Jesus Christ. He is the only way, truth, and life. No one comes to the Father except through Him.[49]

The Bible further teaches that it is only in this life in which salvation may be obtained. "It is appointed for men to die once, and after that comes judgement."[50]

God's offer of salvation is for the whole world, but not everyone will be saved. Only those who are obedient to Christ will be saved. Salvation is not for the Devil.

. . . and the devil [Satan] who had deceived them was thrown into the lake of fire and brimstone where the beast and the false prophet were, and they will be tormented day and night for ever and ever.[51]

And I saw the dead, great and small, standing before the throne, and books were opened. Also another book was opened, which is the book of life. And the dead were judged by what was written in the books, by what they had done . . . and if any one's name was not found written in the book of life, he was thrown into the lake of fire.[52]

These scriptures certainly do not agree with the Unification Church idea that all will eventually be saved, including Satan. The Unification Church may have developed a doctrine of sin and salvation which is not disturbing to people (and what can be disturbing in knowing that eventually everyone will be saved?), but it is disturbing to God. By rejecting God's teaching concerning sin and salvation, the Unification Church cannot honestly call itself "an absolutely Christian movement."

## NOTES

1. Condensed from the *Divine Principle*, pp. 65-80.
2. *Ibid.*, pp. 88-89.
3. Belief in this sin may explain the alleged early practice in the Unification Church of Moon's sleeping with the female converts to purify them.
4. The Unification Church teaches that Jesus removed the problem of the spiritual fall, but did not provide salvation for the physical fall. This idea will be developed more fully in the book.
5. Neil A. Salonen, "A Statement," February 23, 1976, p. 7.
6. This idea and the following example of Jacob are taken from a taped interview with Susan Reinbold and Dan Holdgreiwe at the Unification headquarters in New York City, January 13, 1977.
7. Examples of God's failure, according to the Unification Church, would be His failure with Adam and Eve, Cain and Abel, and Noah—just to name a few.
8. This belief leaves the Unification Church open to all kinds of attack. They may claim that their people do not deceive people when fund raising or recruiting, but how can we know for sure they aren't deceiving people

to fulfill God's will?

9. This is the old "ends justify the means" routine.
10. *New Hope*, p. 71.
11. *Divine Principle*, p. 104.
12. *Ibid.*
13. *Ibid.*, p. 223.
14. *Ibid.*
15. *Ibid.*, p. 140.
16. Young Oon Kim, *Unification Theology & Christian Thought*, p. 103.
17. *Divine Principle*, p. 145.
18. *Ibid.*, p. 142.
19. *Ibid.*, p. 148.
20. *A Prophet Speaks*, p. 127.
21. *New Hope*, p. 45.
22. *Divine Principle*, pp. 224-26.
23. Although the salvation is identical to Jesus' salvation, they teach this is only partial, not full, salvation.
24. *Divine Principle*, p. 225.
25. Kim, p. 165.
26. *A Prophet Speaks*, p. 150.
27. Kim, p. 167.
28. *Ibid.*
29. Gen. 2:18.
30. Gen. 1:31.
31. Gen. 2:25. Italics added.
32. Gen. 3:1-6.
33. Gen. 2:16-17.
34. I Jn. 3:4.
35. Jas. 1:13-14.
36. Rom. 5:12.
37. Ezek. 18:20.

38. Acts 2:23 NIV.
39. Acts 2:38 NASB.
40. Mt. 12:31.
41. Mt. 1:21.
42. Lk. 19:10.
43. 1 Tim. 1:15.
44. Jn. 19:30.
45. Acts 4:12.
46. 1 Tim. 2:5-6.
47. 1 Jn. 1:7.
48. Heb. 10:11-12.
49. Jn. 14:6.
50. Heb. 9:27.
51. Rev. 20:10.
52. Rev. 20:12, 15.

## SIX

# Mission of Christ, Marriage or Cross?

Even though the Unification Church denies the full deity of Jesus, they do admit that he was the Christ, the Annointed One sent by God to accomplish a mission of vital importance. This chapter will examine their concept of Jesus' divine mission and whether or not he was successful in that mission.

What was Jesus' divine mission? According to the Unification Church, Jesus came as another Adam to restore Eden,[1] and to establish a physical kingdom on earth.[2] Reverend Moon says this kingdom was to be established within Jesus' own lifetime.[3]

These statements are certainly straying from a sound

biblical position. If Jesus had intended to establish a physical kingdom on earth during his lifetime, why would he
tell Pilate, "My kingship is not of this world; if my kingship
were of this world, my servants would fight . . ."?[4] Jesus'
rule or kingship was heavenly in origin, not earthly, and
the kingdom itself was heavenly. Throughout the gospels
Jesus speaks constantly of the "kingdom of heaven" (in contrast to an earthly kingdom). When the multitudes were
miraculously fed with the five barley loaves and two fish,
they tried to take Jesus by force to make him their earthly
king, but he withdrew himself from them.[5] He did not
consider an earthly kingship to be his divine mission.

When Jesus said, "My kingship is not of this world," the
"world" of which he spoke referred to the temporal, passing
order of things, that which can decay. This world is con-
trasted with Jesus' kingdom "where neither moth nor rust
consumes. . . ."[6] So when Jesus said that his kingship was
not of this world, he contradicted another doctrine of the
Unification Church, for they teach that in the restored
Garden of Eden people will still die and objects will still
grow old and decay.

The Unification Church teaches that Jesus was to establish this physical kingdom through the perfect family. Since
original sin entered the world through Satan's nature being
passed to Eve sexually, all of their children were born with
this evil element called original sin. In order to remove
original sin, the perfect man (Jesus) must marry the perfect woman and have children, who would automatically be
born without any taint of sin. Their children would repopu-
late the earth, and by this process God's kingdom would be
established.[7]

Referring to marriage in general the *Divine Principle*

teaches that true perfection can only be accomplished within the bonds of marriage.[8] But Jesus Christ was never married. So was he perfect? The *Divine Principle* also states that Jesus was perfected both in flesh and spirit,[9] without explaining how he could be perfected outside of marriage.

They would teach that the Holy Spirit served as the bride of Jesus in a spiritual sense, showing his spiritual perfection. But there is no explanation the authors have learned to show how they could teach that one must be married to be perfected in the flesh, and yet say that Jesus was perfected in the flesh apart from marriage. (Really they cannot say that the Holy Spirit served as the bride of Jesus, because in the first place, in the Greek the term Holy Spirit is neuter and in the second place, masculine pronouns are used to refer to the Holy Spirit.[10]

They explain that before Jesus had the opportunity to marry the perfect woman (if one existed), he was crucified, and God's plan was effectively thwarted,[11] for it was not Jesus' intention to die on the cross.[12] Part of their rationale for making this anti-scriptural statement is that God did not need 4,000 years for preparing for Jesus' crucifixion, since a tribe of barbarians could have slain him even faster.[13]

These are absurd statements when compared with the biblical record. Paul explains that Jesus came at the perfect time, "But when the time had fully come, God sent forth his Son, born of a woman . . . ."[14] Jesus himself realized that the time of his death was to fit within God's timetable, and so he carried out his ministry accordingly. Notice the following references from the gospel of John:

1. At the wedding feast in Cana at the start of Jesus' ministry, he said, "My hour has not yet come."[15]

2. At Jerusalem during the feast of Tabernacles, John explains concerning Jesus' enemies, "So they sought to arrest him; but no one laid hands on him, because his hour had not yet come."[16]

3. "These words he spoke in the treasury, as he taught in the temple; but no one arrested him, because his hour had not yet come."[17]

4. After the triumphal entry into Jerusalem, Jesus said, "The hour has come for the Son of man to be glorified."[18]

5. Concerning this hour of glorification, Jesus also said at the same time, "And what shall I say? 'Father, save me from this hour?' No, for this purpose I have come to this hour."[19]

6. "Now before the feast of the Passover, when Jesus knew that his hour had come to depart out of this world to the Father, having loved his own who were in the world, he loved them to the end."[20]

Then Jesus died at the Passover as the perfect lamb of God who takes away the sin of the world.[21] Nothing in the gospel record shows that this was unplanned from the beginning. For this hour he had come.

The cross stands at the center of all New Testament theology. Apart from the crucifixion and the resurrection such words as atonement, propitiation, salvation, baptism, forgiveness, and life lose their power, and such words have no uniquely Christian meanings apart from the cross. Without the cross there is no gospel, for the gospel which we preach consists of proclaiming the death, burial, and resurrection of Jesus Christ;[22] yet the Unification Church denies that this was God's intended gospel. They preach another gospel, the gospel that salvation for the world comes from the perfect man and perfect woman having blameless children. Paul pronounces a curse upon the Unification Church for preaching this new gospel; he says, "But even if we, or an angel from heaven, should preach to you a gospel contrary to that which we preached to you, let him be accursed. As we have said before, so now I say again, If anyone is preaching to you a gospel contrary to that which you received, let him be accursed."[23]

It is evident that Jesus from the beginning to the end of his ministry planned to die on the cross. At the first cleansing of the temple Jesus began his public ministry in Jerusalem by declaring to the temple officials, "Destroy this temple, and in three days I will raise it up." John explains that Jesus spoke of the temple of his body.[24] Not long after his Great Galilean Ministry Jesus began to teach his apostles that he must suffer, die, and rise again on the third day. Peter rebuked him for considering this to be his mission in life. Jesus replied, "Get behind me, Satan!"[25] If a member of the Unification Church were to travel miraculously back to that point in history, he might tell Jesus, "But Jesus, you are not supposed to die if you want to accomplish God's purpose. You must marry the perfect wife and have perfect children." Jesus' answer to Peter would apply to him as well, "Get behind me, Satan!" Before Peter's rebuke, when Jesus had explained he "must" die, he used the strongest word for must; he did not say he "might" die or "should" die; he said "it is necessary" that he die.[26]

In defense of their position the *Divine Principle* quotes 1 Corinthians 2:8: "None of the rulers of this age understood this; for if they had, they would not have crucified the Lord of glory."[27] ("This" refers to the wisdom of God which he decreed before the ages for our glorification.) The *Divine Principle* claims that this scripture shows that it was not God's will that Christ should die; however, that is not what this passage says. This passage simply reminds the reader of the spiritual blindness of those responsible for Jesus' death. God, when he sent his son to earth, knew there would be spiritually blind men who would oppose His will; and God intended to take their sinful opposition to His will in crucifying the Christ and turn the consequences of that evil action into something good for man's salvation. It was sinful to kill the Christ; God knew man would sin in this way; therefore, God planned from the beginning to annul the evil effects of this sin; henceforth its effects were to be life-saving. This was God's plan from the beginning.

What does the Unification Church do with the multitude of prophecies concerning the suffering and death of the Christ? (For example, Psalm 22 and Isaiah 53.) They explain that the Old Testament contains two kinds of prophecies, one of a suffering servant and the other of a glorified king. The Jews were given a choice as to which of the two kinds of prophecies they would allow to be fulfilled. Unfortunately, they chose to treat Christ as a suffering servant.

The biblical position, as usual, is quite different from the Unification Church. No prophecy from God can remain unfulfilled. Jesus Christ has fulfilled all the prophecies concerning the suffering servant and the glorified king. Right before his death Jesus said to his apostles, "For I tell you that this scripture MUST be fulfilled in me, 'And he was reckoned with transgressors;' for what is written about me has its fulfillment."[28] After his resurrection Jesus said to his two disciples who traveled to Emmaus, "O foolish men, and slow of heart to believe ALL that the prophets have spoken!

Was it not NECESSARY that Christ should SUFFER these things and enter into his GLORY?"[29] Jesus fulfilled his suffering-servant prophecies when he died, and he fulfilled his glorified-king prophecies when he overcame physical death. Jesus continued to explain to those two disciples: "And beginning with Moses and all the prophets, he interpreted to them in all the scriptures the things concerning himself."[30] He later appeared to all the apostles and said, " 'These are my words which I spoke to you, while I was still with you, that EVERYTHING written about me in the law of Moses and the prophets and the psalms MUST be fulfilled. . . . Thus it is written that the Christ should suffer and on the third day rise from the dead.' "[31] (Emphasis added.)

All prophecies concerning Jesus Christ's suffering and glorification have their fulfillment in him. He has become the "King of kings and Lord of lords."[32] No one can ignore his majesty as king when they read the book of Revelation. It is true that a few prophecies concerning the king remain unfulfilled. A favorite example of this type among Unification Church members is Daniel 7:13, 14, which describes the son of man coming with the clouds of heaven to receive rule over all nations of the earth. This scripture can be explained by classifying it with another prophecy yet unfulfilled, delivered at Jesus' ascension into heaven: "Men of Galilee, why do you stand looking into heaven? This Jesus, who was taken up from you into heaven, will come in the same way as you saw him go into heaven."[33] A cloud took Jesus out of their sight,[34] and he will return with the clouds of heaven. Notice the prophecy says that Jesus himself will return, automatically dismissing the idea that any other Christ was needed to fulfill that prophecy; only Jesus can do it. When Jesus returns again, every prophecy concerning himself will have been fulfilled.

## NOTES

1. *Unification Theology & Christian Thought,* p. 91.
2. *Ibid.,* p. 93.
3. *A Prophet Speaks Today,* p. 140.
4. Jn. 18:36.
5. Jn. 6:15.
6. Mt. 6:20.
7. *Unification Theology & Christian Thought,* p. 103.
8. *Divine Principle,* p. 56.
9. *Ibid.,* p. 60.
10. Jn. 16:7-14.
11. *Unification Theology & Christian Thought,* p. 250.
12. *Ibid.,* p. 98.
13. *A Prophet Speaks Today,* p. 135.
14. Gal. 4:4.
15. Jn. 2:4.
16. Jn. 7:30.
17. Jn. 8:20.
18. Jn. 12:23.
19. Jn. 12:27.
20. Jn. 13:1.
21. Jn. 1:29.
22. 1 Cor. 15:1-4.
23. Gal. 1:8,9.
24. Jn. 2:19-22.
25. Mt. 16:21-23.
26. Mt. 16:21.

27. *Divine Principle*, p. 145.
28. Lk. 22:37.
29. Lk. 24:25,26.
30. Lk. 24:27.
31. Lk. 24:44-46.
32. Rev. 19:16.
33. Acts. 1:11.
34. Acts 1:9.

# SEVEN

# The Resurrection, a Ghost of a Chance

According to the *Divine Principle*, since Jesus met an untimely death, he was able to accomplish only "spiritual salvation" for mankind.[1] This is really not enough, because salvation must cover both body and spirit.[2] Therefore, they wait for a new Christ which can provide physical salvation. (This salvation of the body does not mean saving a body from physical death and decay. It means, rather, that bodies will have the taint of "original sin" removed, and men will establish the physical kingdom of God on earth, living in righteousness and peace, making tremendous scientific and technological advances for mankind's betterment.)

The idea of only "spiritual salvation" by Jesus is foreign

to the New Testament scriptures. Jesus has not only saved the spirits of his followers; he has also saved their bodies from the finality of physical death when he was resurrected. The ideas of "spiritual" and "physical" salvation cannot be separated. The apostle Paul, after describing the great resurrection day when Christians' bodies and spirits will be joined together to be with Jesus Christ forever, says, "Therefore comfort one another with these words."[3] In that great day not only will Christians' bodies be raised imperishable, but all of the created universe will be delivered from the curse of futility in which it lies as a result of the fall.[4]

It is ironic that the Unification Church teaches that Jesus Christ only accomplished spiritual salvation, and so God must send another Christ to provide physical salvation. Their physical salvation does not include saving people from the death and decay of their bodies. All changes and improvements in the world are brought about by human scientific achievements. So actually their concept of physical salvation is far inferior to the physical salvation already provided for Christians in the scriptures. When Jesus Christ returns, the perishable bodies of Christians will be changed into "imperishable" bodies,[5] and "the creation itself will be set free from its bondage to decay."[6] Which concept of physical salvation is higher, the Bible's or the *Divine Principle*'s? Since God will not contradict himself, one must decide which concept is from God. Since the *Divine Principle* states that the Bible is from God, and the Bible contradicts the *Divine Principle* on this point, it is safe to trust in the biblical position.

Now all that has been said concerning the biblical position of physical salvation is dependent upon whether or not Jesus himself overcame physical death. Was he bodily

raised from the dead? The Unification Church teaches that
Jesus' resurrection was not physical but spiritual only.[7] For
them the resurrection simply means to advance in growth
and perfection.[8] So when Jesus after his untimely death
appeared to his apostles, he was only a spirit, and physical
eyes could no longer behold him.[9] Yet somehow he was rec-
ognizable, because the spirit is identical to the physical
form.[10]

No Unification Church member can believe in the bodily
resurrection of Jesus Christ and still remain faithful to their
official position. Yet one section of the *Divine Principle*
totally contradicts their own doctrine on this point when
they teach that Jesus appeared to his disciples after his
resurrection in a form exactly identical to that of his lifetime,
and they cite Mt. 28:9 as proof.[11] The scripture cited in the
*Divine Principle* at the end of this quotation refers to Jesus'
resurrection appearance to several women who came to the
empty tomb three days after his death. It says, "And they
came and took hold of his feet and worshipped him." Now
the feet of a spirit cannot be held. This section of the
*Divine Principle* aligns itself with the New Testament account and against its own official position.

The resurrection appearances were meant to prove to
Jesus' disciples that he was physically raised from the dead.
The tomb was empty. The body was gone. Jesus appeared to
his apostles, and they were afraid, thinking they beheld a
ghost, a mere spirit; but Jesus said, "See my hands and my
feet, that it is I myself; handle me, and see; for a spirit has
not flesh and bones as you see that I have."[12] Jesus'
body disappeared from the tomb; it could be touched; it
could eat food; it had flesh; it had bones.

So how can the Unification Church claim that the resurrection of Jesus was only spiritual? Is it because Jesus could appear and disappear at will? Is it because Jesus could hold people's eyes from recognizing him if he so desired? These evidences do not mean that Jesus was only a spirit. They simply show that his perishable body was translated into flesh and bones that would no longer be perishable or bound by time and space.

Finally, did Jesus accomplish his mission fully? He was able to cleanse his followers from all sin.[13] He, by the example of his own physical resurrection, has proven that he is saving both the spirits and bodies of Christians.[14] He has shown that he will rescue the created universe from the futility which binds it.[15] All that Jesus has not yet accomplished, he is able to accomplish and will accomplish at his return.

Yet Reverend Moon has said that Jesus cannot complete God's work of restoration.[16] Young Oon Kim adds that even though Jesus may have thought he failed, this thought was discreetly removed from all gospel records by the original authors.[17]

Professor Kim has discredited her scholarship by making that statement. If the idea of failure is expunged from the record, then so is her evidence for this statement. She is basing her argument upon materials which she herself claims cannot be found within the record. Although she attempts to base her case upon the various gospel recordings of Jesus' words from the cross, she can find no evidence from the earliest gospel to the last that Jesus considered himself a failure in any way.

Professor Kim further states that Christians were anxiously awaiting the return of Christ so that he could finish what he had said and done the first time.[18] She would not only have Christians believe that Jesus considered himself at least a partial failure, but she would also have them believe that the disciples held a similar feeling about Jesus' ministry and so dishonestly changed the historical accounts to cover over their sense of failure.

Jesus was born "when the time had fully come";[19] he died at the right time—"for this purpose I have come to this hour";[20] he will come again at the right time.[21] When Jesus upon the cross cried, "It is finished,"[22] he was not confessing defeat but was proclaiming victory. All that had been his earthly mission found its glorious consummation in that atoning death. He was the sacrificial lamb of God who took away the sin of the world. Victory, not defeat, is proclaimed in the one and only gospel of Jesus Christ the Lord.

## NOTES

1. *Divine Principle*, p. 113.
2. *Ibid.*, p. 147.
3. 1 Thess. 3:13; 4:13-18.
4. Rom. 8:18-25.
5. 1 Cor. 15:54 (also, all of 1 Cor. 15).
6. Rom. 8:21.
7. *Unification Theology & Christian Thought*, p. 134.
8. *Ibid.*, p. 312.
9. *Divine Principle*, p. 360.
10. *Ibid.*, p. 61.
11. *Ibid.*, p. 509.
12. Lk. 24:39.
13. 1 Jn. 1:9.
14. 1 Thess. 4:16,17.

15.  Rom. 8:18-25.
16.  *New Hope*, p. 65.
17.  *Unification Theology & Christian Thought*, p. 99.
18.  *Ibid.*, p. 118.
19.  Gal. 4:4.
20.  Jn. 12:23-27.
21.  2 Pet. 3:9,10.
22.  Jn. 19:30.

# EIGHT

# The Lord of
# the Second Advent

As one investigates the Unification Church's concept of God's purpose for mankind's history, he will discover it differs significantly from the biblical concept. The *Divine Principle* teaches that the purpose of human history is to restore the Garden of Eden.[1] God has searched diligently for a man who will restore the kingdom on earth to Him.

In this work of restoration a definite pattern can be followed. The Unification Church teaches that since there was a 2,000-year time span from Adam to Abraham and 2,000 years from Abraham to Jesus, there must also be 2,000 years from Jesus to the coming of the Lord of the Second Advent, who will complete the work of restoration. They also teach

79

that this 2,000-year Christian era must have six periods of history to coincide with the six periods of the Jewish era.[2]

The section of the *Divine Principle* entitled "Formation and Length of Each Age in the History of Providence" explains this doctrine most completely. No section of the Bible can be compared with this section of the *Divine Principle* in explaining mathematically God's guidance through history. There is no evidence that only 2,000 years transpired from Adam to Abraham; all major evidence seems to point to a far greater time span, one impossible to determine in the depths of antiquity. The classification of six parallel periods of life are forced into unnatural categories, deliberately distorting time spans to fit into their "Chart of the Age of Providential Time-Identity."[3]

During this restoration work the Roman Catholic Church played an important role.

> Christianity became the state religion. Thus Rome came to occupy the position of the Second Israel physically and received the blessing of God.
>
> At that time God expected the Papacy and Rome to completely unite and unselfishly build the unified world left unaccomplished at the time of Jesus.[4]

It is interesting that a religious system which had strayed so far from basic New Testament principles was to be the means by which God would establish his physical kingdom.

Since the "dignity of the Papacy fell,"[5] God raised the British Empire to world prominence, and she should have become a "United Kingdom of God";[6] however, because she persecuted the Puritans and Protestants, a new land of hope was sought. That land was America. So God's plans for

America are great in reestablishing the Garden of Eden. Reverend Moon says that America, God's chosen and beloved nation, must be the model for the kingdom of God on earth.[7]

The *Divine Principle* also explains that the period of preparation for the new messiah began with the Reformation and ended at the close of World War I in 1918.[8] So the new messiah entered the historical scene sometime after 1918.

The whole purpose of this complicated and detailed explanation of historical parallels and interpretations is to show that "the time of the Lord's Second Advent," which they call the "Last Days,"[9] has arrived. The foundational premise of their new religion is that God must send a new Christ, the Lord of the Second Advent, to reestablish Eden. God, they teach, had originally sent Jesus "as the second Adam,"[10] but now the Lord of the Second Advent arrives "as the third Adam."[11]

Can a third Adam exist within God's plans? The apostle Paul refers to Jesus Christ as the "last Adam"[12] or "final Adam." There is no room for another Adam according to the New Testament. Nevertheless, the *Divine Principle* is centered around restoration of the Garden of Eden by a third Adam. If Paul's statement is from God, then the *Divine Principle*'s cannot be, for they totally contradict each other on this point.

What kind of person is the Lord of the Second Advent supposed to be? He will be one who attains sinless deity.[13] He will then produce sinless children who will need no savior to redeem them.[14]

Many believe Reverend Moon considers himself to be this Lord of the Second Advent. In a rare interview with *Newsweek*, international edition, Reverend Moon was asked if he were the new Messiah. He answered, "We are in a new Messianic age. But 2,000 years ago Jesus Christ never spoke of himself as a Messiah, knowing that would not serve his purpose. I am not saying, 'I am the Messiah.' "[15]

It is interesting that this reputed prophet of God knows so very little about Jesus' own claims concerning himself. When the woman at the well said to Jesus, "I know that Messiah is coming (he who is called Christ)," Jesus answered her, "I who speak to you am he."[16] This was at the beginning of his ministry. Later in his ministry Jesus' enemies confronted him, saying, "How long will you keep us in suspense? If you are the Christ, tell us plainly." Jesus told them, "I told you, and you do not believe."[17] During his trial, the High Priest asked him, "Are you the Christ, the Son of the Blessed?" Jesus replied, "I am."[18] Other plain statements to this effect can be found in Jesus' teachings, but these serve as proof that throughout his ministry Jesus openly confessed that he was the Messiah (Christ) and did not correct anyone who called him by that title.

Reverend Moon claims that Jesus never called himself the Messiah, but Jesus' own testimony reads differently. Here is only one example where the prophet from Korea is caught in his own lies. But why would Reverend Moon make such a lie? By not publicly committing himself to being the Messiah, Reverend Moon attempts to insure against an untimely death (like Jesus'), so that he can complete his messianic responsibilities.

When the authors have repeatedly asked a variety of Unification Church members if they believe Reverend Moon to be the Lord of the Second Advent, many avoid giving any kind of answer. Others say that they "dare to even hope that he is." A few, after being questioned thoroughly on the subject, say that they firmly believe him to be the new Messiah. One member the authors questioned at the Unification Church headquarters in New York said that he was sure Reverend Moon was the Lord of the Second Advent. He said he had been at the World Rally for Korean Freedom where Reverend Moon had addressed a crowd of over a million people outside Seoul. The young man described in glowing terms how the cloudy skies opened when Reverend Moon rose to speak, and sunshine descended upon him. At that moment the young man knew he was in the presence of the Messiah. Whether or not such a change in the weather occurred, the authors have not verified, but they were sure of the young man's conviction as to who his great prophet is.

Does Reverend Moon really consider himself to be the Lord of the Second Advent? It would appear that he does, although he makes few public statements to that effect. The new Messiah was to be born in Korea[19] after 1918,[20] according to the post-dated prophecies; Reverend Moon was born in Korea in 1920. He has allowed his disciples to publish the following statement concerning his supremacy:

> . . . he became the absolute victor of heaven and earth. The whole spirit world bowed down to him on that day of victory. . . . The spirit world has already recognized him as the victor of the universe and the Lord of creation.[21]

Concerning his marriage in 1960 to Hak Ja Han, Young Oon Kim wrote, "At that time, the marriage of the lamb, prophesied in the 19th chapter of Revelation took place. Thus, the Lord of the Second Advent and His Bride became the True Parents of mankind."[22] That Reverend Moon and

his wife consider themselves to be the true parents of mankind was made obvious when they officiated at a mass wedding of 1800 couples in 1975, Reverend and Mrs. Moon
dressed in royal attire with beautiful crowns upon their
heads.[23] Therefore, is it any wonder Reverend Moon would
present such a stern warning to America's Christians that
rejecting him could also mean rejecting God.[24]

Now that the Lord of the Second Advent has arrived
(according to the Unification Church), what does the future
hold for the consummation of his work? A third world war
must inevitably come[25] where the communistic world (centering on Stalin, who was the symbolic representation of the
Lord of the Second Advent on the Satanic side)[26] will be
in violent conflict with America and other democratic nations. Democracy will win, and from the rubble a new order
will be established, a socialistic society centering on God.[27]
Within their futuristic framework they teach that God has
no intention of devastating the earth with fire, because this
would imply that God had decided against reconciling humanity or that His creation had been a big mistake.[28]

Contrast their futuristic look with biblical prophecies of
a worldwide cataclysmic destruction:

All the host of heaven shall rot away, and the skies roll
up like a scroll.[29]

But the day of the Lord will come like a thief, and then
the heavens will pass away with a loud noise, and the
elements will be dissolved with fire, and the earth and
the works that are upon it will be burned up.[30]

Then I saw a new heaven and a new earth; for the first
heaven and the first earth had passed away.[31]

According to Reverend Moon this new Garden of Eden will be the kingdom of heaven on earth, for the kingdom must first be physical. To support his statement with scripture (a not too common occurrence), he quotes Jesus' statement, "Whatever you bind on earth shall be bound in heaven, and whatever you loose on earth shall be loosed in heaven." Reverend Moon's explanation of Jesus' statement to Peter is that the kingdom of God must first be established on earth before the kingdom of heaven can exist.[32] This is a strange interpretation for one who claims to be a true prophet of God. If he were a true prophet, the Spirit of God would have revealed to him that the phrase "shall be bound" is a perfect passive participle in Matthew 16:19 in the original Greek New Testament and would most literally be translated "shall be as having been bound." So Jesus' statement can best be understood if read as follows, "Whatever you bind on earth shall have already been bound in heaven, and whatever you loose on earth shall have already been loosed in heaven." Jesus was simply explaining to Peter that Peter's work on earth would follow the pattern of that which had already been established in heaven. Jesus was the heavenly cornerstone of the kingdom, and all foundational apostolic doctrine could only be laid in proper relation to the cornerstone. The apostles did not create a new order of things; they simply passed on what the Lord of the heavens decreed.

Nevertheless, the *Divine Principle* holds that God's heavenly kingdom is still vacant,[33] meaning that no one is there, not even Jesus. The Lord of the Second Advent must establish the kingdom on earth first and then later in heaven. The *Divine Principle* explains the idea this way: The Lord of the Second Advent must establish the kingdom of heaven on earth first, and then when he dies, his spirit will establish the kingdom of heaven in the spirit world.[34] If all that Reverend Moon has said here be true, then Jesus' promise from the cross cannot possibly be true. Remember the thief who said, "Jesus, remember me when you come in your kingdom."[35] Jesus replied, "Truly, I say to you, today you will be with me in Paradise."[36] Jesus here equates Paradise with his heavenly kingdom and said that he was going there and was taking the thief with him. So according to Jesus' own testimony he went to heaven. The writer of Hebrews claims that Jesus rules from there today.[37] Once again the reader is forced to choose between the teachings of Jesus Christ and the Bible or the teachings of Reverend Moon. One cannot accept the testimony of both.

Since the Unification Church teaches that the kingdom of heaven has not yet been established, they have placed themselves in an embarrassing position. The Unification Church teaches that John the Baptist was a villain and the major cause for the failure of Jesus' ministry. Yet Jesus said, "I tell you, among those born of women none is greater than John; yet he who is least in the kingdom of God is greater than he."[38] If the kingdom has not yet been established, then John the Baptist is still at the top of the list of all the great men who have ever lived, and John remains even greater than Reverend Moon himself until such time as the kingdom be established.

One final observation on this general subject needs to be made. If the Unification Church believes the kingdom of God to be physical, then this explains a multitude of their activities. Charges are made that they are politically oriented. Some even say the Unification Church is merely a front for political influence and financial accumulation. If the Unification Church members believe the kingdom to be earthly, then of course they will be as active as possible politically. Of course they will sell as much candy and flowers as possible so that they will have money to purchase property for their kingdom to ransom it from Satan's possession. Of course they will print an attractive color newspaper for propaganda influence on behalf of this physical kingdom. Every government today likes to have at least one newspaper on its side. All of the problems with tax exemption the Unification Church faces, and charges of political intrigue, stem back to their theology of building an earthly kingdom.

## NOTES

1. *Divine Principle*, p. 110.
2. *Unification Theology & Christian Thought*, p. 250.
3. *Divine Principle*, p. 403.
4. Moon, "America and God's Will," September 18, 1976, delivered at the Washington Monument.
5. *Ibid.*
6. *Ibid.*
7. Moon, "God's Hope for America," June 1, 1976, delivered at Yankee Stadium.
8. *Divine Principle*, p. 449.
9. *Ibid.*, p. 498.
10. *Ibid.*, p. 196.
11. *Ibid.*, p. 256.
12. 1 Cor. 15:45.
13. *Divine Principle*, p. 101.
14. *Ibid.*, p. 141.
15. *Newsweek*, international edition, June 14, 1976, p. 48.

16. Jn. 4:25,26.
17. Jn. 10:24,25.
18. Mk. 14:61,62.
19. *Divine Principle*, pp. 519,520.
20. *Ibid.*, p. 449.
21. Bjornstad, *The Moon Is Not the Son*, p. 31.
22. *Ibid.*, p. 62. Tadaaki Shimmyo, translator of *The Divine Principle Study Guide*, Part II, states in his preface that the book was finished February 16, 1975, "on our True Parents' birthday."
23. *Sun Myung Moon*, p. 33, n.d.
24. Moon, "God's Hope for America," June 1, 1976, delivered at Yankee Stadium.
25. *Divine Principle*, p. 491.
26. *Ibid.*, p. 483.
27. *Ibid.*, p. 444.
28. *Unification Theology & Christian Thought*, p. 285.
29. Is. 34:4; Rev. 6:13,14.
30. 2 Pet. 3:10.
31. Rev. 21:1.
32. *A Prophet Speaks Today*, p. 143.
33. *Divine Principle*, p. 176.
34. *Ibid.*, p. 102.
35. RSV reads "kingly power"; the Greek simply says "kingdom."
36. Lk. 23:42,43.
37. Heb. 1:3,13.
38. Lk. 7:28.

# Bibliography

*The Holy Bible, Revised Standard Version.* New York: National Council of Churches, 1973.

Brodie, Fawn. *Thomas Jefferson, An Intimate History.* New York: Bantam Books, 1974.

Bjornstad, James. *The Moon Is Not the Son.* Minneapolis: Dimension Books, 1976.

*Divine Principle*, 2nd edition. Washington, D.C.: Holy Spirit Association for the Unification of World Christianity (HSAUWC), 1973.

"The Divine Principle and the Bible," a debate between the authors and two Unification Church leaders, recorded at the West Islip Church of Christ, Long Island, N.Y., March 8, 1977.

Jones, W. Farley, ed. *A Prophet Speaks Today (the Words of Sun Myung Moon).* New York: HSAUWC, 1975.

Kim, Young Oon. *Unification Theology & Christian Thought,* revised edition. New York: Golden Gate Publishing Co., 1976.

Moon, Sun Myung. "America and God's Will." Sermon delivered at Washington Monument Sept. 18, 1976.

Moon, Sun Myung. "God's Hope for America" (sermon delivered at Yankee Stadium June 1, 1976). New York: Bicentennial God Bless America Committee, 1976.

*Newsweek* (International Edition), June 14, 1976.

Salonen, Neil. "A Statement." January 12, 1976.

Salonen, Neil. "A Statement." February 23, 1976.

Salonen, Rebecca, ed. *New Hope (Twelve Sermons by Sun Myung Moon).* Washington, D.C.: HSAUWC, 1973.

Shimmyo, Tadaaki, translator. *The Divine Principle Study Guide, Part II.* New York: HSAUWC, 1975.

"Sun Myung Moon". New York: Unification Church of America, n.d.

Tape recorded interviews the authors made with Unification Church members at the National Headquarters in New York City.

Vine, W. E. *An Expository Dictionary of New Testament Words.* Old Tappan: Fleming H. Revell Co., 1966.

Yamamoto, J. Isamu. *The Puppet Master.* Downers Grove: InterVarsity Press, 1977.

All royalties from the sale of this book go to Christian Communications of Connecticut, Inc., for the advancement of the gospel proclamation. Address: 495 Park Ave., Bloomfield, Connecticut 06002.